This book is lovingly
dedicated to:

Published by Prism Insight
1959 North Haven Rd
Suite 223
Winston Salem, NC. 27106
loveknowt.com

Book Cover designed by Aqila Teen

Graphic Design by Aqila Teen

1st edition 2023

YOUR BABY NEEDS AN
Auntie Like Me
a GIFT BOOK FOR a NEW MOM from a DEAR FRIEND

a LoveKnowt
Written & Designed by
Agila Teen

Just the
other day
I heard some
great news.

It seems you'll
be buying
some new
baby shoes.

And new baby clothes
and tiny things so sweet.
I can just imagine
Tiny baby feet.

And sweet baby hair

So fine and wispy

And sweet baby's breath

When they lean in

to kiss me.

Then suddenly
it struck me at once
I want to be there
to welcome
its presence.

That was when I knew.
It was so plain to see.
Your baby needs
An auntie like me.

Yes, I know

You have many other friends

But they don't share

Our same confidence.

Our memories

and our good times

The things we shared

Are one of a kind.

They touched my heart then

And they still do

They make me smile

When I think of you.

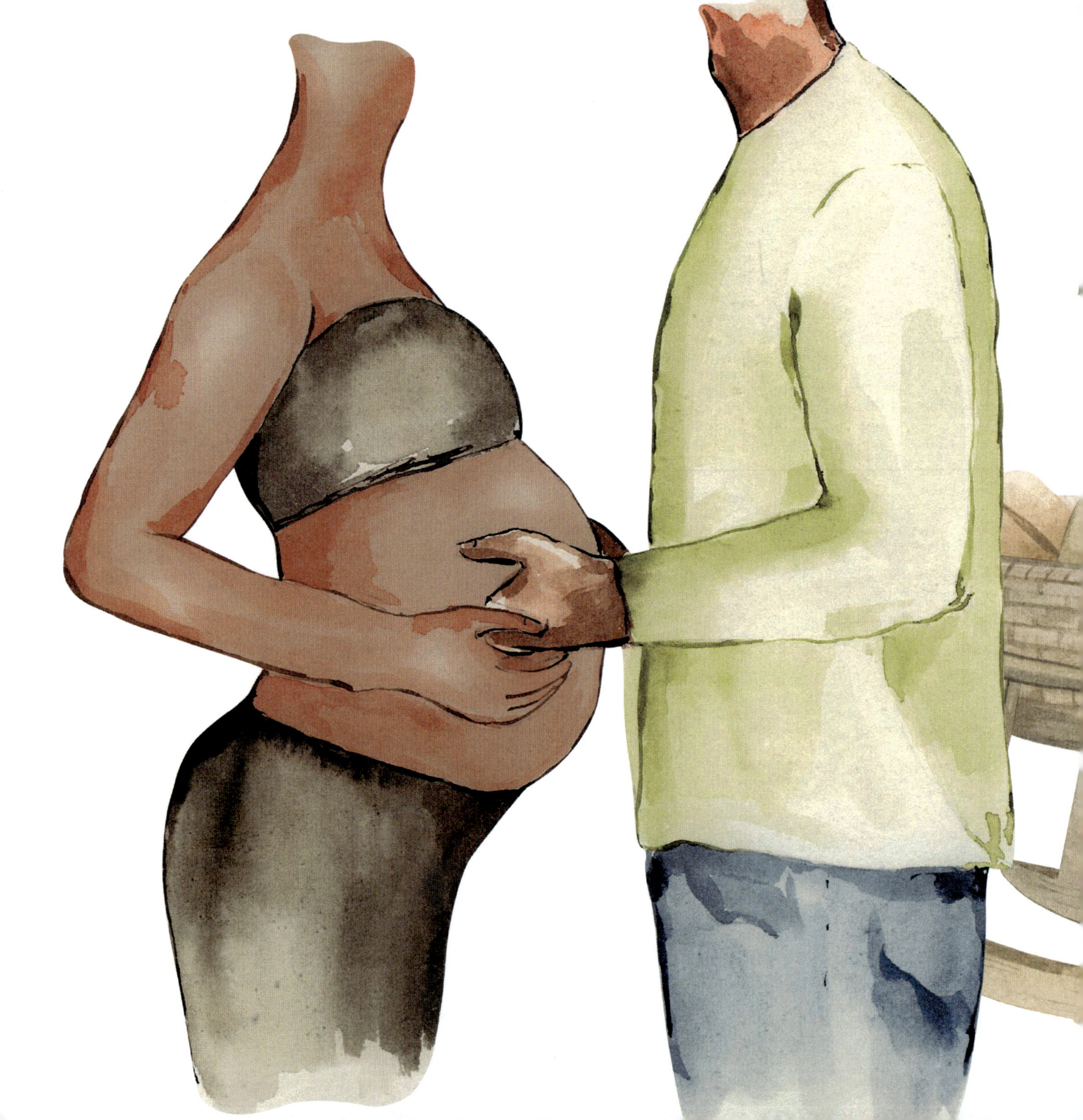

So as you prepare
For life
as a mommy,

I hope to witness
Your growing tummy.

To feel the first kicks
And count 10 little toes.
To buy loads of diapers
And change tiny clothes.
Yes, it's true; and plain
To see. your baby needs an
Auntie like me.

Yes, I know

You have many other friends

But they don't share

Our same confidence.

Our same things to see

And our good vibes

The things we'll share

Will be one of a kind.

Memories I can't wait to share...

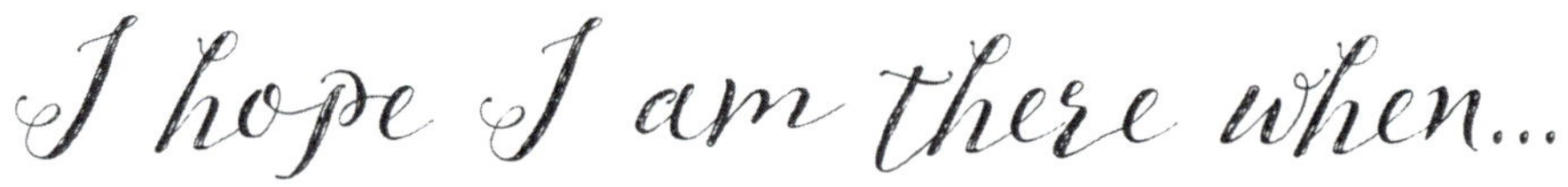
I hope I am there when...

Things I hope we can do...

I'd love to help them learn...

I hope we can...

Made in the USA
Middletown, DE
05 July 2024